black movie

black movie

Danez Smith

Button Poetry / Exploding Pinecone Press
Minneapolis, Minnesota
2015

Published by Button Poetry / Exploding Pinecone Press
Minneapolis, MN 55403

http://buttonpoetry.com

Cover Design: Nikki Clark

ISBN 978-1-943735-00-6

20 21 22 23 24   11 10 9 8 7

TABLE OF CONTENTS

*Because, if I'm honest, people in the white world might be appalled,
but in the black world, they're making myths out of me.
And I know that ain't the life.*

—John Singleton

SLEEPING BEAUTY IN THE HOOD

In the film, townsfolk
name themselves Prince Charming,
queue up to wake the sleeping beauty.

Let's name her Jamal.
Let's make her everyone's brother

or play cousin. All the princes
press a kiss to Jamal's wax-dipped lips.

All the princes sing songs & kill dragons
but Jamal won't wake up.

      You mad? This ain't no kid flick. There is no magic here.
      The fairies get killed too. The kingdom has no king.
      All the red in this cartoon is painted with blood:
      the apples, the velvet robes, Jamal's cold mouth.

BOYZ N THE HOOD 2

Let's not mention the original

nor cast any boyz at all.

The whole thing is a series

of birthday parties for the child

who lives in the picture frame.

Every year we watch his family

light candles on a blue cake.

Every year we watch the family

watch their home burn to the ground.

The movie gets old. The boy never will.

JIM CROW, ROCK STAR

picture him up there!
seersucker cut-offs too tight

cotton shirt freshly picked
& exposed belly, pink cock rocking

a guitar made from your aunt's bones
strung with your great-granddaddy's
stretched out beard.

no fireworks or back up dancers,
he barely sings above a mosquito-wing hum

but you can't turn away, his foot
pressed into the stage like a neck

masked in a hood of blonde curls.
wicked show! when's he's done

you can't even clap, but the encore?

just when you think
the lights are going ghost
he scans the crowd, picks
the youngest brown boy
within reach, hands him
a pistol, whispers

play.

A HISTORY OF VIOLENCE IN THE HOOD

could be a documentary or could be someone's art school thesis
but basically we make a dope ass trailer with a hundred black
children smiling into the camera & the last shot is the wide mouth
of a pistol. We cut on the sound of that gun's hot grey bite
& the preview just keeps repeating over & over
    & the preview just keeps repeating over & over
       & the preview just keeps repeating over & over
    & the preview just keeps repeating over & over
       & the preview just keeps repeating over & over
    & the preview just keeps repeating over & over
       & the preview just keeps repeating over & over
    & the preview just keeps repeating over & over
       & the preview just keeps repeating over & over
    & the preview just keeps repeating over & over
       & the preview just keeps repeating over & over
    & the preview just keeps repeating over & over
       & the preview just keeps repeating over & over
    & the preview just keeps repeating over & over
       & the preview just keeps repeating over & over
    & the preview just keeps repeating over & over
       & the preview just keeps repeating over & over
       & by the end of it, I'm sure some folks will want
their money back
       but I'm sure some will just die for it.
They'll just die.

THE SECRET GARDEN IN THE HOOD

or what happens to dead kids when the dirt does its work

Jonathan, 17, is a blue azalea
sitting in Mary's office.
She waters him every other day.

      Devon, 15, sits on the corner
      dressed in baby's breath.
      His new arms bloom & toes
      tangle with cigarette butts.

Kevin, 19, doesn't hang
out far from his headstone.
He is the greenest grass
in a graveyard that reads
like an attendance sheet.

      Sharlenne, 11, was planted
      yesterday, will be heirloom
      tomatoes by summer.

Mason, 13, was run over
by a 4 year old
barely a bulb himself.

      Kim, 14, went to prom
      pinned to a pinstripe suit.

George, 18, never comes off the porch.

      LaShawn, 9, was rolled up
      & smoked by the busted
      victorious lips of a newly
      crowned Crip.

Kyle, 10, is brown again, dead again.

7

Precious, 11 months
was blown into a wish.

Chucky, 20, made it
to his brother's funeral
laid himself across the casket.

SCENE: PORTRAIT OF A BLACK BOY WITH FLOWERS

& he is not in a casket

nor do I say roses all around him
& mean a low blood tide

he does not return to dirt

the stem does not bloom
from concrete

he does not bring flowers
to his best friend's wake

nor does he give them
to a woman who will
grieve him one day

the boy is in his aunt's garden
& the world does not matter

his lungs are full
of a green, full scent

pollen dusts his skin
gold as he grows

LION KING IN THE HOOD

i. cast list

Mufasa & his absence played by every father ever

Simba played by the first boy you know who died too young

Sarabi played by the woman in church who forgot the taste
of praise once the ground took her son captive

Nala played by the girl crying on the swing for her valentine who
now dates the dirt

Timon & Pumbaa played by Ray-Ray & Man-Man, the joy of not-
dead friends

Zazu played by the ghost of James Baldwin

Rafiki played by a good uncle with a bad habit, his lust for rocks &
stones

Scar played anyone's Uncle June, his ways & his sins & his good
good laugh

The endless rows of hyenas played by a gust
choked tight with bullet shells
the bullets now dressed in a boy

ii. Opening Credits

brought to you by Disney & dead aunts

brought to you on a platter, an apple in the lionboy's mouth

brought to you on a ship bottom reeking of shit & an unnamed sick

brought to you on a tree branch heavy with a tree-colored man

*iii. Opening Scene: The Circle of **[interrupted]** Life*

Nants ingonyama bagithi baba
Sithi uhhmm **[BANG]** ingonyama

Nants ingonyama **[a mother calls for her son]** bagithi baba
Sithi **[BANG BANG]** uhhmm ingonyama

Ingonyama Siyo **[the sound of blood leaving a boy]** Nqoba

Ingonyama **[a mother's knees fall into a puddle
of the blood she made herself]**
Ingonyama **[the slow song of a spirit rising]** nengw' enamabala
[the spirit confused about where its body went]

iv. Song: Oh I Just Can't Wait To Be King

this is the part where they realize that black people dream
& our blood is indeed blood & our teeth, teeth
& the music is loud because the field was wide & long
& we dreamed of simple things: shoes, our children back

this is the part where the racist cuts off his tongue, a wet, pink
      repent
he gives his eyes & his hands & himself to the lions
& the lions feast & the lions are still a metaphor for black boys
& the boys, full of fear turned into dinner, fall asleep & they dream

yes, yes, we really do dream.

v. Song: Be Prepared

for the hands, wild in your wildless hair

for the darkest toll, your double down to get half

to spread your legs while they search for drugs there

for the drug there, for their mouths to ask that big question

for the man, ecstatic with triggers

for the stampede of tiny lead beasts

for the jury not to flinch

vi. Scene: Mufasa Dies at the hands of his brother Scar

What did you expect to be different?
The hood is any jungle (say who? what color the mouth saying?):

a brother kills a brotha

          dark, white birds circling above

*vii. Montage: Timon & Pumbaa teach Simba a music
other than the blues*

clip 1: the boy getting older in spite of everything

clip 2: the boy & the boy-friends smoking blunts
for once something else brown & on fire

clip 3: the boy who would be king with his mouth
in another man's throne

clip 4: Timon & Simba singing
down each other's throat

clip 5: Simba calling Pumbaa a faggot & they all laugh

clip 6: murals of all the dead friends' faces

clip 7: funeral songs. small caskets

clip 8: red, blue, periwinkle, yellow, black, & blood-maroon rags

clip 9: flowers & picture frames on the side walk

clip 10: shot of the boys laughing anyway

clip 11: shot of the boys laughing in the sun

clip 12: shot of the boys laughing in the rain

clip 13: shot of them not being shot

viii. Scene: Simba comes home to kill his uncle

again, a black man
kills a black man

roll the credits
I must go weep.

Why does Disney remind us
what we have learned:

       - one black light swallows another so easy
       - killing is unavoidable as death
       - the king's throne is wet with his brother's blood
       - the queen suffers too but gets no name

ix. closing credits

say the name
of the first boy
you love
who died.
say it
& don't cry.
say it
& love
the air
around your tongue.
say it
& watch
the fire come.
say it
& watch the son rise.

AUTO-PLAY

please get the video of the black man's murder off my timeline I know it happened & my dreams are all the video I need I got to the store & while I knock on the melons listening for ripeness a black man is being killed somewhere there is a white man with hands & whatever he does with them he considers a right white people don't like when you talk about white people because white people think of other white people as not a representation of each other black people call each other brother, sista, fam my nigga I'm thinking about growing my hair out & I'm bout to roll up & every time I open my laptop there is another body drained of a name the name spilled everywhere on everything a mess

SHORT FILM

i. not an elegy for Trayvon Martin

how long

      does it take

a story

      to become

a legend?

how long before

      a legend

becomes

      a god or

forgotten?

ask the rain

      what it was

like to be the river

then ask

      who it drowned.

ii. not an elegy for Mike Brown

I am sick of writing this poem
but bring the boy. his new name

his same old body. ordinary, black
dead thing. bring him & we will mourn
until we forget what we are mourning

& isn't that what being black is about?
not the joy of it, but the feeling

you get when you are looking
at your child, turn your head,
then, poof, no more child.

that feeling. that's black.

        //

think: once, a white girl

was kidnapped & that's the Trojan war.

later, up the block, Troy got shot
& that was Tuesday. are we not worthy

of a city of ash? of 1,000 ships
launched because we are missed?

always, something deserves to be burned.
it's never the right thing.

I demand a war to bring the dead boy back
no matter what his name is this time.

I at least demand a song.   a head.
a song will do for now.

//

look at what the lord has made.
above Missouri, sweet smoke.

iii. not an elegy for Renisha McBride

but an ode to whoever did her hair
& rubbed the last oil into her cold scalp

or a myth of the bullet, the red yolk it hungers to show her

or the tale his hands, pale & washed in shadow
for they finished what the car could not.

if I must call this her fate, I know the color of God's face.

iv. not an ode for John Crawford (a bop)

saint Anthony. please look around. something's been lost and it must be found.
saint Anthony. please look around. something's been lost and it must be found.

story goes homie walked into Wal-Mart
& walked out not born at all.
soon as his hand touched the plastic
them police had a taste for caskets.
& that's all it takes — touch a toy
become not a boy, not a ghost
become a myth that sounds like a lie

saint Anthony. please look around. something's been lost and it must be found.
   saint Anthony. please look around. something's been lost and it must be
     found.

& does it matter his name? John
Hakim, Anthony, Tim,
Ayiende or Fred. I'm scared
to pronounce a man's name if
if soon they'll pronounce him dead.
who fed them this fear or is it human nature
to want to hate the dark? every time they realize
they can't stop the night, another mother buries a son.

   saint Anthony. please look around. something's been lost and it must be
     found.
saint Anthony. please look around. something's been lost and it must be found.

story goes John could have been anybody
as long as he was black, but he was John
had his own scars, his joy, his secret wants
his own mama, his own walk, his own name
& for what? nigga can't go to Wal-Mart without dying?
I try to say my god's name but it just sounds like *vengeance*

24

saint John, saint John. please look around. something's been lost and it must be
    found.
saint John, saint John. please look around. something's been lost and it must be
    found.
saint John, saint John

saint John

        John

                                        John?

v. who has time for joy?

how do you expect
me to dance

when every day someone
who looks like everyone

I love is in a gun fight
armed only with skin?

look closely
& you'll find a funeral

frothing in the corners
of my mouth, my mouth

hungry for a prayer
to make it all a lie.

reader, what does it
feel like to be safe? white?

how does it feel
to dance when you're not

dancing away the ghost?
how does joy taste

when it's not followed
by *will come in the morning?*

reader, it's morning again
& somewhere, a mother

is pulling her hands
across her seed's cold shoulders

kissing what's left
of his face. where

is her joy? what's she
to do with a son

who'll spoil soon?
& what of the boy?

what was his last dream?
who sang to him

while the world closed
into dust?

what cure marker did we just kill?
what legend did we deny

his legend? I have no more
room for grief

for it is everywhere now.
listen. listen to my laugh

& if you pay attention
you'll hear his wake.

//

prediction: the cop will walk free
the boy will still be dead

//

every night I pray to my God
for ashes

I pray to my God for ashes
to begin again

my God, for ashes, to begin again
I'd give my tongue

to begin again I'd give my tongue
a cop's tongue too

vi. not an elegy for Brandon Zachary

a boy I was a boy who took his own life
right out his own hands. I forgot

black boys leave that way too.
I have no words that bring him

back, I am not magic enough. I've tried, but I'm just
flesh, blood yet to spill. people at the funeral

wondered what made him do it. people said
he saw something. I think that's it. he saw something

what? the world? a road?

a river saying his name?

trees? a pair of ivory hands?

his reflection?

his son's?

vii. hand me down

all my uncles are veterans of the war
but most of them just call it blackness.

all their music sounds like gospel
from a gun's mouth. I gather the blues

must be named after the last bit of flame
licking what used to be a pew
or a girl.

I wish our skin didn't come
with causalities, I can't imagine a sidewalk
without blood.

        //

when the men went off to fight
each other, the women stood

in the kitchen making dinner
for white folks. no one said

the kitchen was theirs. no one said
their children didn't thin

then disappear altogether.

        //

not all the women worked
keeping someone else's house in order.
my great grandmother owned her block
a shop where she sold fatback & taffy, ran numbers.

I imagine that little stretch of St. Louis
as a kingdom, a church, a safe house

made of ox tails & pork rinds
a place to be black & not dead.

//

eventually, all black people die.
I believe when a person dies
the black lives on.

viii. not an elegy for...

this one

        nor this one

    nor this one

        nor this one

nor this one

        nor this one

not this one

        nor the next one

nor the one after that

        not this one

    or this one either

no more elegies

    bring the fire

POLITICS OF ELEGY

another brown man is dead
& now he's my ancestor.
I was older than him before
but now he's endless. what
do your people do
with their ghosts? if I write
the name of this new not here
is that the line? what if I write it
with quill & wound? I've trapped
so many boys in poems.
My mouth is an unmarked grave
above which flowers bloom
to sing the dead
or it is just my mouth.
I write about black boys
dying & this woman said
she enjoys my work – what?
failed resurrection? burial?
unsolicited eulogy?
sometimes the boy dying
is me so maybe she means
I'm putting on a good show
so far.

       I won't pin that on her.
I'm the one troubling the water
& calling it mother tears. a flood
is not what it is, but when they –
the loud dead – come for me
I offer them my hands, my pitiful
tongue. that could be a lie. I could be
playing in the corner with my invisible
friends. I say their names & nothing
happens or: I say their names
& a fire starts everywhere or: I say
their names & their names sprout

wings. raise your hands if you think
I'm a messenger. now this time
if you think I'm a tomb raider.
look around. there are no wrong answers.

DEAR WHITE AMERICA

I've left Earth in search of darker planets, a solar system that revolves too near a black hole. I have left a patch of dirt in my place & many of you won't know the difference; we are indeed the same color, one of us would eventually become the other. I've left Earth in search of a new God. I do not trust the God you have given us. My grandmother's hallelujah is only outdone by the fear she nurses every time the blood-fat summer swallows another child who used to sing in the choir. Take your God back. Though his songs are beautiful, his miracles are inconsistent. I want the fate of Lazarus for Renisha, I want Chucky, Bo, Meech, Trayvon, Sean & Jonylah risen three days after their entombing, their ghost re-gifted flesh & blood, their flesh & blood re-gifted their children. I have left Earth, I am equal parts sick of your 'go back to Africa' & 'I just don't see color'. Neither did the poplar tree. We did not build your boats (though we did leave a trail of kin to guide us home). We did not build your prisons (though we did & we fill them too). We did not ask to be part of your America, (though are we not America? Her joints brittle & dragging a ripped gown through Oakland?). I can't stand your ground. I am sick of calling your recklessness the law. Each night, I count my brothers. & in the morning, when some do not survive to be counted, I count the holes they leave. I reach for black folks & touch only air. Your master magic trick, America. Now he's breathing, now he don't. Abra-cadaver. White bread voodoo. Sorcery you claim not to practice, but have no problem benefitting from. I tried, white people. I tried to love you, but you spent my brother's funeral making plans for brunch, talking too loud next to his bones. You interrupted my black veiled mourning with some mess about an article you read on Buzzfeed. You took one look at the river, plump with the body of boy after girl after sweet boi & asked 'why does it always have to be about race?' Because you made it that way! Because you put an asterisk on my sister's gorgeous face! Because you call her pretty (for a black girl)! Because black girls go missing without so much as a whisper of where?! Because there is no Amber Alert for the Amber Skinned Girls! Because we didn't invent the bullet! Because crack was not our recipe! Because Jordan boomed. Because Emmitt whistled.

Because Huey P. spoke. Because Martin preached. Because black boys can always be too loud to live. Because it's taken my father's time, my mother's time, my uncle's time, my brother's & my sister's time, my niece's & my nephew's time... how much time do you want for your progress? I've left Earth to find a place where my kin can be safe, where black people ain't but people the same color as the good, wet earth, until that means something & until then I bid you well, I bid you war, I bid you our lives to gamble with no more. I've left Earth & I am touching everything you beg your telescopes to show you. I am giving the stars their right names. & this life, this new story & history you cannot steal or sell or cast overboard or hang or beat or drown or own or redline or shot or shackle or silence or impoverish or choke or lock up or cover up or bury or ruin

This, if only this one, is ours.

NOTES FOR A FILM ON BLACK JOY

D'Angelo's "Untitled" is on BET, your forehead pressed against the screen trying to look down, praying there's a few more inches of TV. you don't know what drives to you press your skin to the screen filled with his skin but you let yourself be driven, be hungry, be whatever this is when no one is around. you don't know what a faggot is but you know a faggot would probably be doing this. you don't know what a faggot is but you know you might be one. You don't know what you are but you know you shouldn't be. but you know that when D'Angelo sings how he sings looking how he looks, inside you something breaks open & then that odd flood of yes, a storm you can't call a storm but the wind sounds like your name.

////

your auntie & 'nem done finished the wine & put on that Ohio Players or whatever album makes them feel blackest. they dancin' nasty & you watching from the steps when you should be sleep. your uncle is usually a man of much shoulders & silence but tonight he is a brown slur in the light, his body liquid & drunk with good sound. you feel like you shouldn't be looking at how shameless he moves his hips, how he holds your auntie like a cliff or something that just might save him. your mama is not your mama tonight – she is 19 again she unsure what burns in her middle. your not-mama is caught in a rapture so ungospel you wonder if this is what they mean by sin, & if it is, how, like really how, could this be the way to hell? you've never seen her this free, this on fire this - "BOY!" she screams at you but not so you'll go back to bed. she calls you to her, you grab her hands, she shows you where you come from.

////

your grandma sent you out to the big freezer to get some pork chops & while she said they were on top, you can't find them to save your behind. you see neck bones, pig feet, whole chickens,

36

chicken wings, chicken thighs, chicken nuggets, chitterlings, pizzas, freeze pops, some meat you don't know the name of, but not the chops. grandma is gonna have to find it herself. your grandma doesn't have much but she has this. who cares about kingdom if the children don't thin? this was her great northern prayer to make the girls round & winter tough, watch the boys grown broad & alive. glory be the woman with enough meat to let the world starve but not her family, glory the pork chops she sends you to get but you can't find, glory the woman who knows where she placed what is dead & what feeds, who rules the skillet with both hands while both she & the dinner bleed.

//

last summer you weren't bowlegged & your mama noticed you got thick once you shed winter's wool & she damned the young new fat wrapped around her narrow boy & the secret was out: you had secrets & those secrets had hands & mouths & bulges pressed against your jeans in someone else's mama's basement & your jeans are too little & this city was too beige & small for your wild, stay oiled legs to walk & run your mouth to someone's son talking grown & acting like y'all got no home training & oooo he spread you flat & open & arched, your back the black edge of everything, the sun dipping down, look how quick the stars came to spill their barely light everywhere & somewhere on the other side of the horizon inside you a sun falls right out the sky, burns & burns until it pulls back out & you get darker every week in August walking around so black & sassy & unkillable & filled with shine boys look at you & go blind - most with rage, some with hunger.

//

you went to the mall & got errrrythang airbrushed cause homecoming next week. you been practicing the heel-toe for a month now & you need the fit to be as on point. you buy a tall-tee cause you must. you cop some forces cause what else? you didn't buy new jeans but you'll ask your grandma to iron a hard crease how she used to do your church clothes & you expect to be some kind of holy. you bring the tee & the forces & the yet-pressed jeans to the airbrush booth, you want your name in red, your school year down the leg, the shoes with a design almost bloody. & all those little stars that they do for free. so many stars. you gonna be so fly. a sky decked out in ruby.

//

when white folks talk about being black they never talk about how your grandma's brow softens when you raise the spoonful of hot peas to your mouth on New Year's or how your mother called you into her room in the morning to rub lotion on your face when she'd pumped too much. they don't talk about being called into the kitchen to do you dance or sing that little song you sing or just stand there so your mama could be proud in front of company. they won't talk about the rage & terror in her voice when she catches you fighting in the park or with liquor on your breath or anywhere you ain't supposed to be, but are, or the joy she feels when she looks at you, grateful she still has a boy to look at, that no one has tested her joy & succeeded.

DINOSAURS IN THE HOOD

Let's make a movie called *Dinosaurs in the Hood*.
Jurassic Park meets *Friday* meets *The Pursuit of Happyness*.
There should be a scene where a little black boy is playing
with a toy dinosaur on the bus, then looks out the window
& sees the T-Rex, because there has to be a T-Rex.
                    (It's a dinosaur movie, duh)

Don't let Tarantino direct this. In his version, the boy plays
with a gun, the metaphor: black boys toy with their own lives
the foreshadow to his end, the spitting image of his father.
Fuck that, the kid has a plastic brontosaurus or triceratops
& this is his proof of magic or God or Santa. I want a scene

where a cop car gets pooped on by a pterodactyl, a scene
where the corner store turns into a battle ground. Don't let
the Wayans brothers in this movie. I don't want any racist shit
about Asian People or overused Latino stereotypes.
This movie is about a neighborhood of royal folks –

children of slaves & immigrants & addicts & exile saving their town
from real ass Dinosaurs. I don't want some cheesy, yet progressive
Hmong sexy hot dude hero with a funny, yet strong, commanding
Black Girl buddy-cop film. This is not a vehicle for Will Smith
& Sofia Vergara. I want grandmas on the front porch taking out

raptors with guns they hid in walls & under mattresses. I want
those little spitty screamy dinosaurs. I want Cecily Tyson to make
a speech, maybe 2. I want Viola Davis to save the city in the last
scene with a black fist afro pick through the last dinosaur's long,
cold-blood neck. But this can't be a black movie. This can't be a

black movie. This movie can't be dismissed because of its cast
or its audience. This movie can't be metaphor for black people
& extinction. This movie can't be about race. This movie can't be
about black pain or cause black people pain. This movie
can't be about a long history of having a long history with hurt.

This movie can't be about race. Nobody can say nigga in this movie
who can't say it to my face in public. No chicken jokes in this
movie. No bullets in the heroes. & no one kills the black boy.
& no one kills the black boy. & no one kills the black boy. Besides,
the only reason I want to make this is for that first scene anyway:

little black boy on the bus with a toy dinosaur,
his eyes wide & endless

his dreams possible, pulsing, & right there.

NOTES & ACKNOWLEDGMENTS

Dinosaurs in the Hood & subsequently a large portion of the poems in this project owe their creation to & were inspired by Terrance Hayes' "We Should Make a Documentary About Spades."

Dear White America contains lines by Amiri Baraka and James Baldwin.

//

Many thanks to the editors and staff of the following publications in which early versions of these poems have appeared:

Poetry Magazine, At Length, Michigan Quarterly, HEart Journal, Storyscape Journal, Blue Shift,   & Spilt This Rock's Poem of the Week

Thank you Michael Mlekoday & the whole Button Poetry / Exploding Pinecone Team for making this happen. Huge thanks Marcus Wicker for choosing this chapbook for publication and your wisdom which helped craft it.

Thank you everyone in the Dark Noise Collective for your constant and monumental love. Thank you Sad Boy Supper Club for being the weird boy coven I've always wanted. I love you all.

Thank you to Cave Canem, The Poetry Foundation, The McKnight Foundation, and the Millay Colony of the Arts for all the support in making this.

Thank you to black people everywhere for being so beautiful and resilient and wondrous.

Thank you to my grandmamma n' nem. I love you all too much for words.

And thank you, reader.

ABOUT THE AUTHOR

Danez Smith is the author of *[insert] boy* (2014, YesYes Books), winner of the Lambda Literary Award for Gay Poetry. His 2nd full-length collection will be published by Graywolf Press in 2017. His work has published & featured widely including in *Poetry Magazine, Beloit Poetry Journal, Buzzfeed, Blavity,* & *Ploughshares.* He is a 2014 Ruth Lilly - Dorothy Sargent Rosenberg Fellow, a Cave Canem and VONA alum, and recipient of a McKnight Foundation Fellowship. He is a 2-time Individual World Poetry Slam finalist, placing 2nd in 2014. He is the micro-editor for *The Offing* & is a founding member of 2 collectives, Dark Noise and Sad Boy Supper Club. He is an MFA candidate at The University of Michigan. He is from St. Paul, MN.